It is often said the Renaissance began in the city state of **Florence**, which had grown wealthy during the medieval period through banking and the wool trade. As a **republic**, Florence was ruled by a collection of powerful families. The most powerful of these were the Medici, who supported the artist Michelangelo and the great Renaissance figure Leonardo da Vinci (see box). The dome of Florence Cathedral is one of the earliest examples of Renaissance architecture. It was designed by Filippo Brunelleschi, and inspired in part by the Pantheon in Rome.

Another important Renaissance city was the Republic of **Venice**, which dominated Mediterranean trade routes and was the most prosperous city in Europe. A third Renaissance city was Milan. Though not a republic, Milan's ruling family, the Sforzas, transformed it into an artistic and cultural centre to rival Florence and Venice. In Rome, many more ancient statues and buildings were being uncovered. These inspired Renaissance sculptors and architects to copy their styles. This can be seen in the Corinthian columns at St Peter's Basilica in the Vatican, and statues such as Michelangelo's masterpiece *David*, completed in 1504.

Leonardo da Vinci

There were many great Renaissance philosophers, mathematicians, artists and inventers, but one man was all those things and more. His name was Leonardo da Vinci.

Born the illegitimate son of a poor farm girl in 1452, Leonardo began working for the Medici in Florence during his twenties. Aged 31 he moved to work for Ludovico Sforza in Milan. There he completed his masterpiece in 1499, a painting of the Last Supper on the refectory wall of the convent of Santa Maria delle Grazie'.

Leonardo was also a great scientist and inventor, though many of his inventions were never made. His notebooks still exist today, and contain designs for a bicycle, helicopter, parachute and even a solar panel! They also reveal his obsessive struggle to find the fundamental patterns and rules that define human life, leading to his famous drawing of the perfectly proportioned 'Vitruvian Man'. It is sometimes difficult to believe that all of Leonardo's achievements and interests belonged to just one man.

Fact

Brunelleschi also developed the technique for creating **perspective** in artworks by using a vanishing point. Thanks to the use of perspective, Renaissance art is noticeably different to the flatter appearance of medieval paintings.

Completed by Raphael in 1504, this painting is an early example of perspective in Renaissance art.

Check your understanding

1. The rebirth of what cultural activities was said to have started the Renaissance in medieval Europe?

2. How did the fall of Constantinople and the Crusades help spur the European Renaissance?

3. Why were Italian city states so wealthy?

4. How did the artistic technique devised by Filippo Brunelleschi change Renaissance painting?

5. What were some of Leonardo da Vinci's accomplishments?

Unit 2: The age of encounters
Print, gunpowder and astronomy

Under the influence of the Renaissance, scholars increasingly broadened their concerns away from religious learning, and towards the study of mankind.

A new term emerged to describe this development: **humanism**. This change was helped by the growth of universities. The first European university was founded in the Italian city of Bologna in 1088, and universities in Oxford, Paris and Salamanca soon followed. By 1400, there were 53 universities in Europe, where students could study subjects such as law, philosophy, medicine and mathematics.

Printing Press

In medieval Europe, it took a monk up to three years to produce one handwritten Bible. For this reason, books were hugely expensive, and only the very wealthy or the very religious had access to them.

That was until Johannes Gutenberg, a metalworker from the German town of Mainz, started experimenting with printed text. The technology of printing with blocks of carved wood had arrived in Europe from China, but woodblock printing was time consuming and inefficient. Gutenberg's idea was to create equally sized individual letters out of metal that could be arranged and rearranged in a wooden frame to make whole pages of words, a technology known as '**movable-type printing**'. Gutenberg would then cover the metal type blocks with ink, and press onto them a sheet of paper, and then another, and then another.

Replica of an early printing press

In 1455, Gutenberg's **printing press** produced its first run of Bibles: 180 copies, each with 1286 pages. This started a **revolution**. By 1500, there were over 1000 printing presses in Western Europe, producing large numbers of books on religion, medicine, history, poetry, **astronomy**, and Latin grammar, sold at prices that many more than just the wealthy could afford. New ideas could now spread to many more people at an unprecedented speed. It is no coincidence that the Reformation began just half a century after Gutenberg's revolutionary invention.

Gunpowder

Gunpowder was invented in China, and first arrived in Europe during the 14th century.

During the siege of Constantinople in 1453, the Turkish Sultan Mehmed II employed a Hungarian engineer named Orban to build the largest cannon the world had ever seen. Measuring 29-foot-long and nicknamed 'The Imperial', it took a team of 60 oxen to haul Orban's cannon towards Constantinople. Once in position, 'The Imperial' fired stones weighing half a tonne towards

Collins

Key Stage 3
Early Modern Britain

The age of encounters

Robert Peal

Knowing History

The Italian Renaissance

Compared with the scholars of the Islamic world, and the scientific advances of the Song dynasty in China, Europe was not at the forefront of advancing human knowledge during the medieval period.

This situation began to change during the 15th century. Starting in Italy, Europeans took a new interest in the cultural achievements of their **classical** forebears – the Ancient Greeks and Romans. While much classical writing had been forgotten within medieval Europe, it was kept alive by the scholars of the Islamic world and the Byzantine **Empire**. Due to the increased contact with the Islamic world during the Crusades, and the fall of Constantinople in 1453 (see box), classical drama, poetry, science, mythology, philosophy and political thought began to find its way back into Europe.

This led to a period of extraordinary artistic and cultural flourishing in Europe known as 'the **Renaissance**', meaning 'rebirth' in French.

'The School of Athens', painted by Raphael in 1509, depicts the greatest thinkers of the classical world

Fall of Constantinople

The Byzantine Empire never recovered from Constantinople's humiliating sacking by a Venetian-led army during the Fourth Crusade. This sent the city into a spiral of decline. By 1453, what was once the greatest Christian city on earth was surrounded by 100 000 Turkish troops under the command of a brilliant but ruthless Turkish sultan called Mehmed II.

On Tuesday 29th May, Mehmed's troops poured into the city, killing its inhabitants, looting its churches, and turning the Hagia Sofia into a mosque. This led many of Constantinople's artists, priests and scholars to flee for safety in Europe. These refugees brought with them to Europe the books and ideas of Ancient Greece and Rome. Thus, the rebirth of classical civilisation in medieval Europe was spurred by its dying gasps in Constantinople.

Italian city states

While feudal monarchs ruled most of medieval Europe, a small number of Italian cities were different. These were independent **city states**, which governed themselves and their surrounding area, and were able to develop a distinctive character of their own. As urban centres, the Italian city states were home to Europe's most successful trade guilds, craftsmen, merchants and bankers – making them extremely wealthy. The city state's most powerful figures demonstrated their importance by becoming **patrons** of the arts, sponsoring the work of painters, architects and writers.

View of Florence, and its famous domed cathedral

the famous city walls of Constantinople. These walls had protected the Byzantines from invasion for a 1000 years, but after sustained cannon **bombardment**, they crumbled.

By the 16th century, gunpowder had conclusively spelled the end of medieval warfare. Faced with canon bombardment, even Europe's most feared castles were defenceless. Armed with a handgun, a lowly foot soldier could shoot dead a knight in shining armour. In 1620, the English scientist Francis Bacon wrote: "Printing, gunpowder and the compass: these three have changed the whole face and state of things throughout the world".

Surviving portion of the walls of Constantinople, in modern day Istanbul

Astronomy

During the Renaissance, the ideas of the Greek astronomer Ptolemy were rediscovered. Ptolemy suggested that the heavenly bodies (sun, moon, planets, and stars) revolved around the earth, something known as a '**geocentric**' theory of space. The Roman Catholic Church welcomed Ptolemy's theory, as it placed God and the earth at the centre of the universe.

However, a number of astronomers observed that the movement of the planets in the night sky was irregular, and they did not appear to orbit the earth. In 1543, Nicolaus Copernicus published a book called *The Revolution of the Heavenly Orbs*. In this book, Copernicus proposed a '**heliocentric**' theory, where the earth and the planets orbit the sun. The Catholic Church saw this as heresy, and banned Copernicus's book. But his troubling idea would not go away.

Galileo Galilei

Galileo Galilei was a mathematics professor from Florence with an interest in astronomy. In 1609, he developed a new technology to observe the night sky: the telescope. Galileo openly supported Copernicus's heliocentric theory of the universe in his university lectures. In 1616 he was summoned to Rome where he was forced to deny his beliefs. Galileo was a committed Christian, so he agreed, but he could not sustain the lie. In 1632, he published *Dialogue concerning the Two Chief World Systems*. This book mocked the arguments of the Catholic Church, and explained Copernicus's heliocentric theory.

Now a frail old man, Galileo was once again summoned to Rome. This time, he was threatened with torture, and after a series of interrogations, Galileo denied that the earth revolved around the sun. For his remaining years, Galileo lived under house arrest, and died in 1642.

> Fact
>
> The Catholic Church only formally ended their opposition to a heliocentric view of the universe in 1835.

Check your understanding

1. The growth of which institutions helped the spread of 'humanism' in medieval society?
2. Why did the invention of the printing press make books cheaper, and more efficient to produce?
3. Why did the invention of the printing press play an important role in the Reformation?
4. How did the use of gunpowder in Europe spell the end of medieval warfare?
5. What did astronomers observe, which made them propose a heliocentric theory of space?

Unit 2: The age of encounters
Global exploration

In medieval Europe, merchants could buy silk, spices and porcelain from faraway lands such as India and China. But merchants almost never visited these countries.

Goods from India and China were carried overland for thousands of miles along the '**Silk Road**'. This was not an actual road. Instead, it was a general route across central Asia, through the Islamic world, through Asia Minor to Constantinople, across the Mediterranean to Italy, and from there to the rest of Europe. The journey took years, during which time goods would have been bought and sold by merchants perhaps a dozen times, each time rising in price. By the time it arrived in Northern Europe, Chinese silk could be worn by only the wealthiest members of the nobility, and black pepper from India was an untold luxury.

Large parts of the Silk Road crossed through deserts, so camel trains were used to transport goods.

If a European merchant wanted to trade directly with India or China, they faced a perilous overland journey lasting years. For this reason, few ever attempted it.

Marco Polo

One exception to this was Marco Polo, the son of a Venetian jewel merchant. Aged just seventeen, Marco Polo set off with his father and uncle in 1271 on a mission to meet the Mongol Emperor Kublai Khan in his new capital city of Beijing. They were given a blessing from the Pope to convert Kublai Khan to Christianity.

Venetian explorer Marco Polo

Twenty-five years later, Marco Polo and his father returned to Venice. In 1298 Marco Polo published an account of his travels entitled *Description of the World*. The book captivated medieval Europe, and became a medieval bestseller. It told the extraordinary story of Marco Polo's journey to Beijing, his work as a military advisor to Kublai Khan, and his return to Europe escorting a Mongol princess to Persia. It also detailed the wealth of riches and luxuries to be found in China.

Ever since its publication, however, people have wondered how much truth there is to Marco Polo's fantastical adventures. Some parts are clearly made up, such as his account of Prester John, a mythical Christian king who never actually existed. As for the considerable time he spent in China, Polo accurately records their use of paper money and coal for fuel, but neglects to mention anything about chopsticks, Chinese characters for writing, or the Great Wall of China. In contemporary sources from all of the locations in China that Marco Polo claims to have visited, there is no single mention of a European advisor to Kublai Khan.

> **Fact**
>
> On his deathbed, Marco Polo's friends begged him to admit that his book was fiction, but he replied: 'I have not told half of what I saw.'

Sailing to India

True or not, it was clear from Marco Polo's stories that a great prize lay in wait for the first European merchant to establish a trading route with East Asia by sea. However, a large obstacle lay in the way: Africa. Navigation had slowly been improving during the medieval period, with the magnetic compass being used from the 13th century onwards. This, and the rediscovery of a description of world geography by the Greek astronomer Ptolemy, inspired an increased interest in sea exploration amongst Europeans.

The keenest medieval explorers were the Portuguese. Throughout the 15th century, Portuguese sailors travelled further and further down the west coast of Africa. None, however, was able to round the treacherous **Cape of Good Hope** at the tip of the African Continent, and sail on to India.

None, that was, until the Portuguese explorer Vasco da Gama, who was chosen to lead an expedition to India in 1497. On 8 July his fleet of four ships and 170 men left Lisbon. Almost one year later, he landed at Calicut in India, where they met the local king and exchanged European goods for a selection of Indian spices. After a horrendous journey home through the Indian monsoon, da Gama landed in Lisbon on 10 July 1499. Only 54 of his men had survived, but that did not matter to da Gama; he had become the first European to successfully sail to, and trade with, India.

In the years that followed, Portuguese sailors established a permanent trading post in Calicut, and terrorised the Muslim merchants who had previously dominated Indian Ocean trade. A new age of trade, **colonies** and empire was being born in Europe.

Portuguese explorer Vasco da Gama

Sir John Mandeville

In 1371, a book was published containing the account of an English explorer called John Mandeville. He reported discovering a tribe who lived off the smell of apples, headless people with faces on their chests, and people with feet so large they used them as shade from the sun. The book was a bestseller, but Mandeville never existed, and his work was an elaborate hoax.

Check your understanding

1. Why were goods from China and India so expensive during the medieval period?
2. What story did Marco Polo's book *Description of the World* tell?
3. What obstacle prevented European merchants from sailing to East Asia?
4. Which country provided the keenest explorers in medieval Europe?
5. What historic feat did Vasco da Gama achieve in 1499?

Unit 2: The age of encounters
Christopher Columbus

Christopher Columbus was an Italian sailor from Genoa with one big idea: finding an alternative route to East Asia.

Contrary to popular myth, it was commonly understood in medieval Europe that the world was round. By this logic, Columbus believed the Indian Ocean could be reached by avoiding the Cape of Good Hope, and sailing due west across the Atlantic.

Known as the 'western passage', Columbus needed funding for his bold idea. He lived in Portugal, but the Portuguese King João II refused to back his voyage, as did the rulers of France, Venice, Genoa and England. Support finally came from King Ferdinand and Queen Isabella of Spain, who gave Columbus the money he required for a crew and three ships.

Statue of Christopher Columbus in Barcelona, Spain

Sea crossing

On 6 September 1492, Columbus set sail from the Canary Islands with 96 men, led by his flagship the *Santa Maria*. Imagine the terror and excitement they must have felt, setting sail across the vast expanse of the Atlantic Ocean and into the unknown.

Using the writings of Ptolemy as a guide, Columbus calculated that Japan lay just 2400 miles away, and would take four weeks to reach. In fact, Japan was 7000 miles away from Europe, and a whole unknown continent lay in between. Four weeks into the journey, Columbus and his men still had not seen land, and they were running out of fresh water. The crew were growing impatient, so Columbus agreed to continue sailing for four more days before turning home. Two days later, a sailor named Rodrigo de Triana sighted land.

Arrival in America

On 12 October, Columbus landed on the small Caribbean island of Guanahani. There, he found a peaceful **native** people called the **Taíno**, who did not wear clothes, and spent their lives farming, fishing, and smoking rolled up leaves of a then unknown plant called tobacco. Columbus sailed on to the nearby island of Hispaniola, where he found native people wearing small items of gold jewellery.

Columbus left 39 men on Hispaniola, and set sail back for Spain bringing with him evidence of his discovery to show Ferdinand and Isabella: gold jewellery, chilli peppers, sweet potatoes, parrots, and nine captured natives. Columbus's stories of a new land, and his hopes of finding greater reserves of gold, entranced the Spanish court. Having claimed that it was he, and not Rodrigo de Triana, who

Contemporary engraving of Christopher Columbus landing at Hispaniola in 1492

first sighted land, Columbus was rewarded with a pension of 10 000 silver pieces for every year until his death.

With the support of Pope Alexander VI, Ferdinand and Isabella claimed ownership of all lands discovered across the Atlantic. The Portuguese King João II insisted that Spain should share the spoils, so in 1494 the **Treaty of Tordesillas** was signed. This extraordinary agreement drew a line down the globe running 370 leagues west of the Cape Verde Islands. Anything west of the line belonged to Spain, anything east of the line belonged to Portugal. To this day, most of South America speaks Spanish, aside from an eastern bulge jutting out into the Atlantic called Brazil, which speaks Portuguese.

Columbus's legacy

In later life, Columbus became increasingly religious, and he took to dressing as a monk. Columbus refused to believe that the Bible could have failed to mention an entire continent, so he was never willing to accept that he had discovered a new land. Right up until his death in 1506, Columbus insisted that he had simply found the outer islands of East Asia. Columbus's mistake can still be heard in the language we use today: a string of Caribbean islands are known as the 'West Indies', and native Americans are commonly referred to as 'Indians'.

Modern illustration of Columbus's flagship the *Santa Maria*

Those explorers who followed Columbus would often describe the Americas as 'virgin' territory, meaning an untouched and uninhabited wilderness. This was only true because the native population had no immunity to diseases carried by the Europeans. The arrival of European settlers in the Americas caused an unintended genocide of catastrophic proportions.

Historians estimate that 90 percent of the native American population at the time of the European arrival died from new diseases such as measles, smallpox, malaria, and tuberculosis – perhaps 75 million in total. As for the Taíno, the Caribbean people who Columbus first encountered, within 18 years 99 percent of their population had perished. All that survives of them is a handful of words from their native language that are still in use today: canoe, hammock and barbecue.

Fact

Columbus was not the first European to reach America. Historians now agree that the Vikings got there nearly 500 years previously, but they never established permanent settlements.

Check your understanding

1. What route did Christopher Columbus believe he could take to sail to East Asia?
2. What did Columbus find when he landed on the island of Guanahani?
3. What was decided between Spain and Portugal by the Treaty of Tordesillas?
4. How is the error Columbus made when he discovered America reflected in words we use today?
5. Why did so many of the native people of the Americas die after Europeans made first contact?

Unit 2: The age of encounters
The 'New World'

Columbus's journey across the Atlantic blew the world wide open. Soon a constant stream of explorers was sailing from Portugal and Spain to explore these lands further.

In 1502, an Italian explorer, Amerigo Vespucci, who was working for the Portuguese sailed south along the coast of Brazil to the tip of **Patagonia**. Vespucci concluded that this was no outlying Asian island, but a whole new continent. When he returned to Lisbon in the spring of 1503, Vespucci wrote a letter to his friend, a member of the Medici family in Florence. Vespucci explained that Columbus was wrong, and that the land across the Atlantic was a '**New World**'.

The conquistadors

From 1516, Spain's ruler Charles V authorised further exploration of the American mainland, and his Spanish explorers became known as **conquistadors**.

In 1519, a conquistador named Hernán Cortes sailed from Cuba with 600 men, 16 horses and 14 cannon to explore the American mainland. Cortes arrived in Mexico, ruled at the time by the great **Aztec** Empire. Their capital was Tenochtitlán, a magnificent city of 200 000 inhabitants, built on an island in the middle of a lake. The Aztec emperor Montezuma had no reason to fear Cortes' piffling force, so he invited them into his city. Here, Cortes found enormous, unimaginable stockpiles of gold.

Ruined pyramids built by a native Mexican civilisation before the arrival of European settlers.

Relations between the Aztecs and the Spanish soured, and Montezuma was killed. Cortes fled the city, and returned in April 1521 with a much larger invasion force. Though the Aztecs were fearsome warriors, they were still a Stone Age civilisation. Cortes's army had steel swords, handguns and cannon, whilst the Aztecs had arrows, slings, and clubs made with sharpened volcanic stone. Cortes defeated the Aztecs, destroyed Tenochtitlán, and built a new, European style city in its place.

A similar story occurred when a Spanish conquistador called Francisco Pizarro landed in Peru, then ruled by another great civilisation, the **Inca** Empire. This time, European diseases had reached the native population before the Europeans themselves, and the Incas were ravaged by smallpox. In one of the most famously uneven battles in human history, Pizarro managed to defeat an Inca force of 80 000 with just 168 men, thanks to the panic and confusion caused by his cannon and galloping horses. The Incan emperor agreed to buy off the Spanish with rooms full of gold and silver.

Ruins of Machu Picchu, a citadel built by the Incas on a mountain ridge, abandoned around the time of the Spanish Conquest.

Global trade

In the age of global exploration, Spain had won the lottery. Before long, a continual supply of gold and silver was flowing from their South American colonies to the Spanish crown. As well as precious metals, the discovery of the New World brought new foods such as tomatoes, potatoes, chocolate, peanuts and vanilla, and new luxuries such as tobacco.

In countries where the local population was harder to subdue, the Spanish and Portuguese established coastal trading stations instead of colonies. Known as factories, these spread along the coasts of West and East Africa, India, China, Malaysia, Indonesia and the Philippines (named after Mary I's husband King Philip II of Spain). Portugal and Spain would dominate overseas trade for most of the 16th century, building the world's first truly global empires.

Map of the world, created in France in 1566

Ferdinand Magellan

In September 1519, a Portuguese sailor working for the Spanish set sail with five ships and 265 men for Indonesia, then known as the Spice Islands. Ferdinand Magellan plotted an audacious route heading west not east, intending to be the first European to sail around the tip of South America.

Magellan sailed towards Patagonia, where he claimed to encounter a race of giants, twice the size of Europeans. He then found a narrow channel leading to the other side of the continent. Freezing cold and beset with storms, the Magellan Strait, as it became known, is a dangerous route to sail. One ship sank, and another turned back. But after 38 days, Magellan and his men came out the other side, reaching an enormous ocean, which seemed calm in comparison. So they called it the Pacific, meaning 'peaceful'.

In March 1521, Magellan and his men reached the Philippines, where a local chieftain asked them to help him in a war against a rival tribe. Magellan agreed, but was killed by poisoned arrows during the battle. In September 1522, a single ship from Magellan's original expedition finally returned to Spain, with just 18 surviving men on board. However, they had earned their place in history as the first crew to **circumnavigate** the world.

Check your understanding

1. How did America gain its name?
2. How did the Pacific Ocean gain its name?
3. What advantages did Hernán Cortes and his conquistadors have when fighting the Aztecs?
4. Why were the Inca already weakened by the Europeans before Pizarro arrived in Peru?
5. What sort of goods, which are common in Europe today, originated in the New World?

Unit 2: The age of encounters
Knowledge organiser

1498 Leonardo da Vinci completes 'the Last Supper'

1453 The fall of Constantinople

1492 Christopher Columbus crosses the Atlantic and lands in America

1455 The Gutenberg bible is printed in Mainz

1494 Spain and Portugal sign the Treaty of Tordesillas

1499 Vasco da Gama returns from his voyage to India

Key vocabulary

Astronomy The science of studying extraterrestrial objects, and the universe

Aztec Native American civilisation who ruled much of what is today called Mexico

Bombardment To attack continuously a place with missiles until it gives way

Cape of Good Hope The southern tip of Africa, notorious for its stormy weather and rough seas

Circumnavigate To sail around something, often used to mean sailing around the world

City state A political system where a single city governs itself and its surrounding territories

Classical Relating to the art, culture or history of Ancient Greece and Rome

Colony A country or area under the political control of a foreign country

Conquistadors Spanish soldiers who led the conquest of the Americas

Empire A group of countries or states presided over by a single ruler

Florence Italian city state and banking centre where the Renaissance was said to have begun

Geocentric A system in astronomy where the earth is at the centre of the universe

Heliocentric A system in astronomy where the sun is at the centre of the universe, or solar system

Humanism A system of thought which concentrates on the human realm, often in place of religion

Inca Native American civilisation who ruled much of what is today called Peru

Movable-type printing A system of printing that uses and rearranges individual letters and punctuation

Native A person born in, or historically associated with, a particular country or region

New World Term given to North and South America following Columbus's voyage in 1492

Patagonia Region at the southern tip of the South American continent

Patron Someone who gives financial support to a person or institution, most often an artist

Perspective A method in art of depicting three-dimensional objects, often using a vanishing point

Printing Press A revolutionary invention, first created by Johannes Gutenberg around 1455

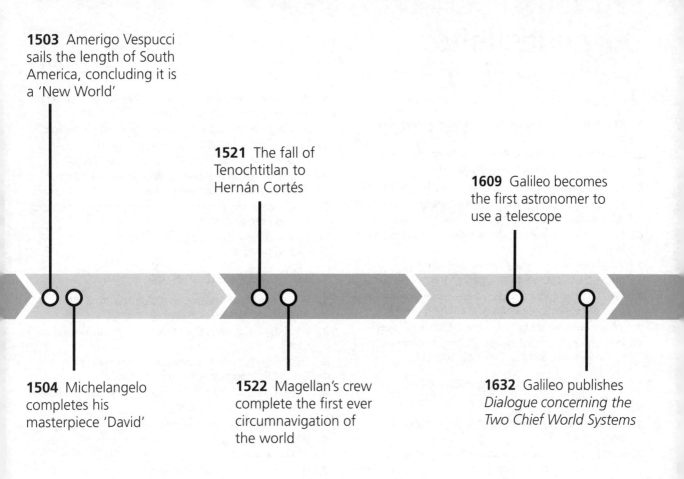

1503 Amerigo Vespucci sails the length of South America, concluding it is a 'New World'

1521 The fall of Tenochtitlan to Hernán Cortés

1609 Galileo becomes the first astronomer to use a telescope

1504 Michelangelo completes his masterpiece 'David'

1522 Magellan's crew complete the first ever circumnavigation of the world

1632 Galileo publishes *Dialogue concerning the Two Chief World Systems*

Key vocabulary

Renaissance Literally meaning 'rebirth', a period of cultural flourishing in late medieval Europe

Republic A state where the ruler is not a monarch, but comes from amongst the people

Revolution A change which means that nothing will ever be the same again

Silk road An ancient overground trade route which linked East Asia with the west

Taíno The native people of the Caribbean, wiped out by European diseases

Treaty of Tordesillas A treaty that divided the new world between Spain and Portugal

Venice City in northern Italy that dominated Mediterranean trade during the medieval period

Key people

Christopher Columbus Explorer who crossed the Atlantic and claimed the land he encountered for Spain

Filippo Brunelleschi Renaissance architect and artist who pioneered the use of perspective

Galileo Galilei Italian astronomer who supported a heliocentric theory of the universe

Hernán Cortes Spanish conquistador who defeated the Aztecs

Johannes Gutenberg German publisher who introduced movable-type printing to Europe

Leonardo da Vinci Renaissance genius who painted the Last Supper

Marco Polo Italian explorer who wrote a bestselling medieval book about his journey to China

Mehmed II Turkish sultan who conquered Constantinople

Vasco da Gama The first European to establish an overseas trading route with India

Quiz questions

Chapter 1: The Italian Renaissance

1. Which part of the world kept classical writing alive during the medieval period?
2. What does 'Renaissance' mean in French?
3. In what year was the Fall of Constantinople?
4. Which Turkish sultan conquered Constantinople?
5. What do you call a political system where a single city governs itself, such as medieval Venice?
6. In which Italian city was the Renaissance said to have begun?
7. What do you call a state where the ruler is not a monarch, but comes from amongst the people?
8. What artistic method depicts three-dimensional objects on a flat surface, often using a vanishing point?
9. Which Renaissance genius painted the *Last Supper*?
10. In what city did this Renaissance genius spend much of his later career, and paint the *Last Supper*?

Chapter 2: Print, gunpowder and astronomy

1. The first European example of what was founded in Bologna in 1088?
2. What system of thought concentrates on the human realm, often in place of religion?
3. In what year was the first bible produced in Europe using a printing press?
4. Which German publisher built Europe's first printing press?
5. What system of printing uses and rearranges blocks of individual letters and punctuation?
6. A 29-foot-long canon nicknamed 'The Imperial' was used to lay siege to which city?
7. What did the Catholic Church believe lay at the centre of the universe?
8. What system in astronomy places the sun at the centre of the universe, or solar system?
9. Which Italian astronomer deduced that the earth revolves around the sun, by observing the orbit of the planets?
10. How was this Italian astronomer punished by the Catholic Church after 1632?

Chapter 3: Global exploration

1. What ancient over-ground trade route linked East Asia with the west?
2. What happened to products traded from East Asia to Europe, each time they changed hands?
3. Which 13th century Italian explorer wrote a bestselling book about his journey to China?
4. Who did this Italian explorer claim to have worked for during his time in China?
5. What significant structure did this Italian explorer fail to mention in his account of China?
6. Which country produced the keenest medieval explorers?
7. What is the name of the southern tip of Africa, notorious for its stormy weather and rough seas?
8. Which European explorer established Europe's first overseas trading route with India?
9. What goods did this European explorer return to Lisbon with after reaching India?
10. Where in India did Portugal establish a permanent trading post?

Chapter 4: Christopher Columbus

1. In what year did Christopher Columbus cross the Atlantic and land in America?
2. What Italian city was Christopher Columbus originally from?
3. The king and queen of what country supported Columbus's journey across the Atlantic?
4. When he set sail across the Atlantic, what continent was Columbus trying to reach?
5. What was Columbus's flagship called?
6. Which native people of the Caribbean did Columbus first encounter?
7. Name two items which Columbus brought back with him to show Ferdinand and Isabella?
8. What treaty divided the new world between Spain and Portugal?
9. What mistaken belief did Columbus hold onto until his death in 1506?
10. What percentage of the Native American population are estimated to have died due to European diseases?

Chapter 5: The 'New World'

1. The continent of America was named after which Italian explorer?
2. What were the Spanish soldiers who led the conquest of the Americas called?
3. Which Spanish conquistador led the conquest of Mexico?
4. Which Native American civilisation ruled much of what is today called Mexico?
5. In what year did the city of Tenochtitlan fall to the Spanish?
6. What European disease had already weakened the Inca civilisation before the conquistadors fought them?
7. What is a country or area under the political control of a foreign country called?
8. What is a group of countries or states presided over by a single ruler called?
9. Who was the first sailor to circumnavigate the world in 1522?
10. What sea was named during the 1522 circumnavigation of the world, meaning 'peaceful'?

William Collins' dream of knowledge for all began with the publication of his first book in 1819. A self-educated mill worker, he not only enriched millions of lives, but also founded a flourishing publishing house. Today, staying true to this spirit, Collins books are packed with inspiration, innovation and practical expertise. They place you at the centre of a world of possibility and give you exactly what you need to explore it.

Collins. Freedom to teach

Published by Collins
An imprint of HarperCollins*Publishers*
The News Building
1 London Bridge Street
London SE1 9GF

ISBN 978-0-00-819536-6

Publisher: Katie Sergeant
Editor: Hannah Dove
Author: Robert Peal
Fact-checker: Barbara Hibbert
Copy-editor: Sally Clifford
Image researcher: Alison Prior
Proof-reader: Ros and Chris Davies
Cover designer: Angela English
Cover image: © Victoria and Albert Museum, London
Production controller: Rachel Weaver
Typesetter: QBS
Printed and bound by Martins, UK

Acknowledgments

Every effort has been made to trace copyright holders and to obtain their permission for the use of copyright material. The publishers will gladly receive any information enabling them to rectify any error or omission at the first opportunity.

The publishers would like to thank the following for permission to reproduce copyright material:

(t = top, b = bottom, c = centre, l = left, r = right)

Cover & p1 © Victoria and Albert Museum, London; p2t Aristotle and Plato: detail of School of Athens, 1510–11 (fresco) (detail of 472), Raphael (Raffaello Sanzio of Urbino) (1483–1520)/Vatican Museums and Galleries, Vatican City/Bridgeman Images; p2b kavalenkava volha/Shutterstock; p3 The Marriage of the Virgin, 1504 (oil on panel), Raphael (Raffaello Sanzio of Urbino) (1483–1520)/Pinacoteca di Brera, Milan, Italy/Bridgeman Images; p4 Dja65/Shutterstock; p5t dinosmichail/Shutterstock; p5b Everett - Art/Shutterstock; p6t Nithid/Shutterstock; p6b North Wind Picture Archives/Alamy; p7 Classic Image/Alamy; p8t imageBROKER/Alamy; p8b Everett Historical/ Shutterstock; p9 Michael Rosskothen/Shutterstock; p10t Anna Omelchenko/Shutterstock; p10b KasperKay/ Shutterstock; p11 Planisphere by Nicolas Desliens; 1566/De Agostini Picture Library/Bridgeman Images; p12 Classic Image/Alamy

Collins

Key Stage 3
Early Modern Britain
The age of encounters

The Knowing History unit booklets help you to:

- Think critically about the past by focusing on the knowledge you need and then checking your understanding.

- Learn history through extraordinary people, amazing facts, and a distinctly engaging narrative.

- Remember key dates, vocabulary and significant people with the 'Knowledge organiser'.

- Test your knowledge with 'Quiz questions' for each chapter.

Knowing History Early Modern Britain booklets

Henry VIII and the Reformation 978-0-00-819532-8
The age of encounters 978-0-00-819536-6
The later Tudors 978-0-00-819533-5
The English Civil War 978-0-00-819534-2
Commonwealth and Restoration 978-0-00-819535-9
Georgian Britain 978-0-00-819537-3

The Early Modern Britain booklets are also available in:
Early Modern Britain 1509–1760 Student Book 2

Medieval Britain
410–1509
Student Book 1
978-0-00-819523-6

Early Modern Britain
1509–1760
Student Book 2
978-0-00-819524-3

Modern Britain
1760–1900
Student Book 3
978-0-00-819525-0

Free Teacher Guides available on www.collins.co.uk

Collins
FREEDOM TO TEACH

Find us at **www.collins.co.uk**
and follow our blog – articles and
information by teachers for teachers.
🐦 @FreedomToTeach

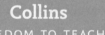

ISBN 978-0-00-819536-6

9 780008 195366 >